VIRAGO

THE WOMAN OF HUES

LEKSHMI S

To My World,

for the love, patience and unwavering belief in my craft.

Contents

1. BLOOM

It must pour, it must root....

My lilies scented sweet memories
of pleasant mornings
Let them be mine forever....

Scented Lilies

Freshly bloomed

Painted canvas in the corner

Their fragrance

calms and comforts,

Twirling gently like fairies in the breeze.

I whispered my tale to them,

These innocent posies

among dark leaves,

Handing me the charm of love.

Oh lilies, May I rest upon you?

Lost in thought,

They laid their petals over me.

Embrace your love

with a smile of hope..

Phases of Smile

A tiny seed of light,

blinking eyes with a gentle smile.

So close to the heart,

shifts like changing seasons

Silence ! to the fairy cheers.

Cheeks blush with

a fiery hue, not a grin to embrace,

confused to love, treat and

echo the smile.

Rhythm of life changes,

chasing fleeting dreams

too hurried to share a smile

leaves life empty.

The smell of earth when rains

evoke warmth within us..

From Petrichor

I met myself today,

and i named her Petrichor.

she refreshes everyone

only when the first rain

falls upon the earth.

Her scent, so often missed

amidst the wild chaos.

But if you sit quietly

listening to her whispers,

You will find she longs for you

to breathe her in again.

only then you realize-

she has always existed.

Be selfless to seek the highest

and give love freely..

Agape

Your heart longs for a beloved,

once bound a vow:

"Commitment without Conditions"

How magical!

The soul found its love

and thus begins, lub dub.

Each beat echoes a promise.

A rhythm that never fades

in the twilight.

Love, so pure and deep,

fills the sacred space

with calm and ease.

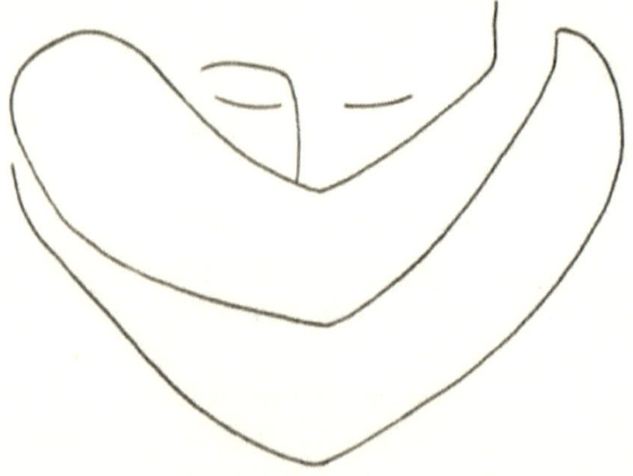

Find your inner peace,nurture your soul...

A Cup of Self Love

Fill your cup everyday

with self love

and add some peace

to your life

you deserve your

love the most

let it pour into your

empty cup and spill

with sweetness.

Embrace serene mornings

sit among the flowers

let your smell makes

them bloom.

find yourself

and the art in you.

2. GROW

It must begin, it must grow....

At home, we sit and enjoy
serene memories are treasured parts..

Homecoming

We don't miss those

phosphene catches and late

night talks, the smell of

brewing coffee that kept us

together.

We didn't know that we were

making memories.

Slowly we are meant to leave

the things that we hold.

But coming back to where

you started is a magic.

Shades of woman shift and twist

healing blends with

yet love means a lot to her...

Virago

Its from the broken

that we bloom into

different shades of love.

We smile even in

the very next pluck

of pain, which

heals the lessons of

wound once

turned red.

She has many colours

to grow out

for the best change.

Trust her love

her colours.

Here you are safer

stay close to me

until i fall...

Blooming belly

A seed once started

dancing in my belly.

Soon grown roots in my heart.

I poured it with delight and

waited for the darling bud.

Bless me for the sacred life.

Before long, our beautiful

thoughts planted with hope

bloomed out to be a tiny little

blossom.

Together we weave our love

and happiness.

Even in darkness we find our solace...

Together in Turmoil

You are the pearl in my shell

safely placed with love

no matter what storm arises,

you stand loyal to my side

holding my pain of disruption.

Within the essence of our life,

we created our happiness.

In the face of turmoil

we have learned and

grown to steady ourselves

never hear the noise

of others words

Let them speak,

Let them judge,

but never let it

anchor your soul.

Whether its dawn or dusk

beauty remains constant...

Sigh

Yes! It is defined

from the strand of hair

to the crack of toe.

Wrap your face

turn aside to those

raw words.

Morning chants may

depress you but

rise from those rays.

Do not tweak your skin.

Let the rooter pick

gems from the pores.

Sonnet 18 to

Shall i compare thee to Dusk.

Which shines so long.

A confused mind always

drifts in thought,

it is in haze at times...

Trauma Bond

Many feel so high,

and down when it matters.

Give and take - mere illusions

when loyalty falters

as a fragile thread worn upon

the crown of expectations.

Reward them as outcast!

quiet , forgotten souls

yearning for a place to belong.

Memory of hurt,

makes them glum.

In seeking peace and self care

they find strength to

call out for love.

Accept fragility in

your own times

to rediscover ourselves..

The Untold

A girl once loved everyone

comforted, cared and empathized

never sat still for herself,

but treated others with joy

tucking away her own needs

and smiling behind the veil.

She gave and shared

carried the weight of worries

and lessen the load of them.

Chaos shaped her into a rebel

neither calm or quiet within

wrangling with the world and herself

reformed into someone new.

amidst the storm

still she loved

she cared.

3. DREAM

It must fade, It must revive..

A cycle of old gives way to new
recreate, renew, replicate...

Rebirth

Soak your eyebrows

in the briny deep,

Let your tears fall free,

And relax into the

endless world of blue.

where the old self fades

unravel the knots of pain

and dead scales of burden,

from the depth, rise

a new life, fresh as lily.

Dive into the light above,

swipe away those evil eyes

burn them with your glow.

Breathe in the scent of purity

and tread yourself to a world

refreshed by the deep blue sea.

Bloom and grow...

Elysian

My palette of red and pink

rests softly on the cot,

As i step into my cozy room

where every corner inhales

the warmth of painted love

I gently placed my canvas on the

wall lighted up by the golden rays.

Took some yellow, green and white

splashed them across the frame,

the colours began to dance with the

brush turned out as a glimpse of beauty.

That pride of pleasure knows no end..

Then i crawled into my bed embracing

the eternal realm of my dreams.

Peace comes from within..

Peace

Be you ! honest and true

never let the women laugh

at who you are trust yourself

be you!

Stand firm and forgive

gain strength not shame

find peace, root yourself

be you!

Bestow the cherished memories

to those unseen shadows, blanket

them with your belonging.

be you!

Remember men are men

And women are women!

www.ingramcontent.com/pod-product-compliance
Lightning Source LLC
Chambersburg PA
CBHW021813150726
47989CB00004B/1913